MW00628984

More Praise for *Consider the Turkey*

"This small but powerful book is full of riveting facts, including some jaw-droppers. Readers will be left wondering how, if cruelty to animals is a crime (and it is), anyone can be excused for subjecting a turkey to a raft of pain and misery so that he—invariably he—can be reduced to a carcass for the carving. *Consider the Turkey* promises to convert many a Thanksgiving dinner into a celebration of life."

—Ingrid Newkirk, president of People for the Ethical Treatment of Animals (PETA)

"In *Consider the Turkey*, renowned ethicist Peter Singer delivers a striking indictment of humanity's treatment of other animals. Poultry industry marketing would have us believe that we purchase happy and humanely raised and slaughtered turkeys for Thanksgiving. But what looms in the

(CONTINUED)

background is a system that disregards the dignity of humans and other animals and poses an existential threat to all of us. Singer's work highlights the need for fierce moral courage by leaders who will enact policy that prioritizes compassion for all species, including our own."
—Crystal Heath, DVM, executive director of the veterinary advocacy organization Our Honor

"This short but revelatory book recounts in harrowing detail all that is done to turkeys during their brief lives before they are killed and eaten. I fervently hope that it will be widely read and that the awakened compassion of ordinary people will prove stronger than the rapacity and cruelty of the leaders of the turkey production industry."
—Jeff McMahan, University of Oxford

CONSIDER
THE TURKEY

CONSIDER

the

TURKEY

Peter Singer

PRINCETON UNIVERSITY PRESS

Princeton & Oxford

Published by Princeton University Press
41 William Street, Princeton, New Jersey 08540
99 Banbury Road, Oxford OX2 6JX

press.princeton.edu

Library of Congress Cataloging-in-Publication Data

Names: Singer, Peter, 1946– author.
Title: Consider the turkey / Peter Singer.
Description: Princeton : Princeton University Press, [2024] |
    Includes bibliographical references.
Identifiers: LCCN 2024018093 (print) | LCCN 2024018094 (ebook) |
    ISBN 9780691231686 (hardback) | ISBN 9780691231693 (ebook)
Subjects: LCSH: Animal welfare—Moral and ethical aspects. |
    Thanksgiving Day. | BISAC: PHILOSOPHY / Ethics & Moral
    Philosophy | COOKING / Vegetarian
Classification: LCC HV4708 .S564 2024 (print) | LCC HV4708 (ebook)
    | DDC 179/.3—dc23/eng/20240520
LC record available at https://lccn.loc.gov/2024018093
LC ebook record available at https://lccn.loc.gov/2024018094

British Library Cataloging-in-Publication Data is available

Cover Art: Victoria / Adobe Stock; Endpaper Art: bubaone /iStock

This book has been composed in Fraunces

Printed in the United States of America

10 9 8 7 6 5 4 3 2 1

Contents

CONSIDER
THE TURKEY

Chapter 1

Pardoning Turkeys— All of Them

The United States has many strange practices, but one of the oddest is surely the annual ritual of "pardoning" a turkey before Thanksgiving. Although President Abraham Lincoln is said to have spared a live turkey who had been brought home for Christmas dinner, presidential pardons for turkeys go back only 60 years. As with so many US practices, this one began with a clever marketing idea: the National Turkey Federation presented a live turkey to President Harry S. Truman for Thanksgiving dinner. The presentation made the media, and after that it became an annual event. In 1963, President John F. Kennedy received a turkey who had, draped around his neck, a sign saying, "Good Eating, Mr. President." Face-to-face with the turkey, the president said, "We'll just let this one grow." His immediate successors didn't follow his example, but President George H. W. Bush did, and from then on, every president has continued to "pardon" a turkey, or sometimes two turkeys, just before Thanksgiving.

The US Constitution authorizes the president to grant a pardon for a federal crime, but no one has ever suggested a crime for which the turkeys are supposedly being pardoned. Presumably that's because turkeys don't commit crimes. Does it make families in the United States feel better, as they chew on the corpse of one of the 46 million turkeys killed annually for Thanks-giving dinners, to know that somewhere, two of them are still alive? Our minds can play strange tricks, especially when we have doubts, perhaps unconscious ones, about the ethics of something we want to do. Could Americans today imagine that the spared turkey carries away the sin of the turkey dinner, as the ancient Hebrews be-lieved that if they let a goat escape into the desert, the "scapegoat" would carry away their sins? Or is it just all a convenient al-liance between the interests of producers in selling more turkeys and those of US presidents in staying on friendly terms with agribusiness? Is it at all relevant that, as we will see in the pages that follow, Jen-nie-O, the supplier of the turkeys pardoned by President Joseph Biden in 2023 and the nation's biggest turkey producer, received nearly $106 million in 2022–24 from the federal government as compensation for the deaths of turkeys it owned—millions of whom it killed slowly, by deliberately heating them to death?

*

How we treat animals is fundamentally an ethical issue, and one that I have been thinking and writing about for more than fifty years. Over that time, we have made some progress, but not nearly enough, and in some respects we have gone backward. Mass turkey production illustrates how things have gone wrong. I do not believe that most people in the United States regard the practices I describe in this book as acceptable, yet by buying and consuming turkey products, they are complicit in them. So my primary motivation for writing the book is to inform Americans about the nature of the bird who is the centerpiece of their most celebrated meal, and about the lives and deaths of the more than 210 million turkeys commercially produced in the United States in 2022. But I hope that the book will prompt people everywhere to inquire into the lives and deaths of the animals traditionally consumed for celebrations, whether it is Christmas, Passover, or Eid.

For many of you, by the time you have finished reading this book, no more ethical argument will be necessary. You will already know that what I describe is wrong. For others, I will, before I close, briefly sketch a simple ethical argument that shows that to support the present industrial system of producing turkeys is wrong.

Chapter 2

"A Tremendously Handsome, Outgoing, and Intelligent Turkey"

Turkeys are birds of the genus *Meleagris*, native to North America. About 20 million years ago, they evolved from the common ancestor they share with pheasants and grouse. Turkeys were first domesticated by Indigenous Americans about 2,200 years ago and became an important source of protein for them. The turkeys that Americans eat today, however, came to the United States by a roundabout route. The Spanish arrived in Mexico in 1519, and it wasn't long before they took turkeys raised by Aztecs to Spain. Over the next 200 years, the practice of raising turkeys for food spread throughout Europe. At first the birds were thought to be guinea fowls, who were known as "turkeys" because they arrived in Europe via Constantinople, then ruled by Turks. Eventually, of course, people realized that the birds from Mexico were quite different from guinea fowl, but the name stuck.

Male turkeys are typically much larger and more colorful than the females. They have a courtship display in which they strut about to show off their fine feathers. During this display, their snood—a fleshy protuberance on their heads—becomes engorged with blood and extends beyond their beak. (Among wild turkeys, females have been shown to prefer males with longer snoods.)

The behavior of male turkeys entered English consciousness sufficiently rapidly for Fabian, in William Shakespeare's *Twelfth Night*, to describe the conceited Malvolio as "a rare turkey-cock . . . how he jets [struts] under his advanced plumes!"

English colonists settling in North America in the eighteenth century brought turkeys with them. Thus the descendants of birds who had evolved and were first domesticated in Mexico came back to North America, but in varieties that had been bred in Europe.

*

It is a common myth that domesticated turkeys are stupid—so stupid, it is said, that if they are outside when it rains, they will look up at the falling rain until they drown! There is no scientific basis for this belief, which is not surprising given that turkeys evolved and survived in regions where rain occurs.

We know that both wild and domesticated turkeys with freedom to roam over an ample area will, like farmyard chickens, live in groups typically consisting of about 20 individuals. Within these groups, hierarchies form. Our expression "pecking order" derives from observations of these hierarchies. Initially, sorting out the hierarchy may involve some pecking from the stronger and more aggressive birds, but eventually the subordinate birds will learn to keep out of the way of those above them in the hierarchy. To do so, they must be able to recognize others in the group and know to whom they must yield, and who they can dominate. Like humans, there is a limit to how many others they can remember and recognize. As a result, and as we will see in chapter 4, fights among turkeys are more common when thousands of birds are crowded into a single shed than when turkeys are outdoors and have sufficient space to form a durable social group.

One widely used indication of cognitive ability in animals is the mirror test, in which animals of various species are accustomed to the presence of a mirror, and researchers then find ways of discovering whether the animals take their own image as a different animal, perhaps an intruder who evokes a hostile response, or instead recognize that they are seeing their own image—thus indicating that they possess self-awareness and see themselves as distinct individuals existing over time. This test works only on animals who have good vision and rely on sight to distinguish between individuals. Dogs, who use their sense of smell more than sight, fail the standard mirror test, but pass an olfactory version of it. But birds do use vision, and an ingenious experiment has shown that roosters pass the mirror test. Roosters warn their fellow chickens of the presence of a predator, but when they are alone they do not give a warning. In the presence of a mirror image of themselves, they do not warn, which indicates that they do not see the image as another rooster.

After reading a report of this experiment, I contacted the lead author, Sonja Hillemacher, seeking information about similar studies on turkeys. "There literally exists no literature on turkey cognition," she replied, but added, "It seems reasonable that turkeys might be able to recognize themselves in a mirror when chickens can, because turkeys have also a very (if not even more) complex social behavior."

Hillemacher did, however, refer me to videos and anecdotal information about Cornelius, a turkey living together with Esther, a pig, on a sanctuary for farmed animals in Ontario. Steve and Derek founded the sanctuary after they adopted Esther, and then other animals started arriving from people who could not care for them. Cornelius, they report, "quickly made himself right at home" by moving from the main barn into the house shared by Steve, Derek, and Esther. A blog post from the sanctuary describes him as "a tremendously handsome, outgoing, and intelligent turkey," and "an incredibly sensitive and loving brother" to the other animals he lives with. Cornelius soon learned the locations of all the food storage containers in the home. According to Derek, "He also has amazing eyesight and can spot a banana being peeled open from across the room. He LOVES bananas and always has count on how many should be in the bowl." Cornelius has an especially close relationship with Esther. When the weather is wet, they stay inside and cuddle up together in some blankets. When Esther had to go to the hospital, Cornelius seemed concerned, and often stood outside, waiting for Esther to return. When Esther finally did come home, there was a joyful reunion with lots of cuddles.

At the time that blog post was written, Cornelius was seven years old, and still healthy and active. As you read the later chapters of this book, try to remember Cornelius and keep in mind that each turkey is an individual, with their own personality as well as the potential to have a life as long and rich as Cornelius had.

*

The United States is the world's largest turkey producer and the largest exporter of turkey products. In 1970, Americans ate just over 8 pounds per person annually; by 2021, that figure had nearly doubled to more than 15 pounds. In 2023, US turkey meat production for the domestic market was estimated to be a little more than 5 billion pounds a year, with another 400 million pounds exported. Minnesota, the state with the highest production, was responsible for 37 million turkeys annually. Ironically, Mexico, where turkeys were first domesticated, is now the largest international market for US turkey producers, taking almost two-thirds of the US turkey exports.

Modern breeding has transformed turkeys. In the 1930s, the average weight of a commercially produced turkey in the United States was 15 pounds. As late as 1960, it was still under 17 pounds. But then selective breeding for size really started to have an impact, and by 2017, the average weight per bird had passed 30 pounds. The broad-breasted white became the dominant breed, accounting for as many as 99 percent of all turkeys sold. As the name implies, birds of this breed have broad breasts—a big marketing plus because most turkey eaters want a slice of the breast. Breeding turkeys to have such a large breast comes with a distinct disadvantage, though, as we are about to discover.

Chapter 3

How to Make a Turkey

The *Merck Veterinary Manual*, a standard online reference work, notes that as "a consequence of large, heavily muscled birds being unable to physically complete the mating process," artificial insemination is routinely used in the turkey industry. The widely used manual then provides a detailed description of how to masturbate a turkey. This is done

> by stimulating the copulatory organ (the phallus) to protrude by massaging the abdomen and the back over the testes. This is followed quickly by pushing the

tail anteriorly with one hand and, at the same time, using the thumb and forefinger of the same hand to apply pressure in the cloacal area to "milk" semen from the ducts of the phallus.

The same manual offers guidance for inserting the semen into the female:

When holding the hen upright, pressure is applied to the abdomen around the vent, particularly on the left side. This causes the cloaca to evert and the oviduct to protrude, so that a syringe or plastic straw can be inserted ~1 in. (2.5 cm) into the oviduct and the appropriate amount of semen delivered. As the semen is expelled by the inseminator, pressure around the vent is released, which assists the hen in retaining sperm in the vagina or oviduct.

This clinical account gives little idea of the reality of artificial insemination for the hen in an industrial production setting in which workers do this, all day, every day. Jim Mason, who grew up on a farm in Missouri, went to law school, and became a lawyer for an animal advocacy organization, decided that the best way to get a sense of what artificial insemination is really like for turkeys and workers is to work as a turkey inseminator. Butterball, America's largest turkey producer and a division of the agribusiness giant ConAgra, was advertising to fill spots on its artificial insemination crews in Carthage, Missouri. Mason applied and was told to turn up at the plant. When he got there, he was asked to take a drug test. Passing that appeared to be the only qualification required because he was hired without ever having been asked a single question about his prior experience with turkeys or artificial insemination.

Mason spent some time on both sides of the job: collecting the semen from the tom, as male turkeys are called, and squirting it into the hen. At the tom house, where the males are kept separately from the females, his role was to catch a tom by the legs, hold him upside down, lift him by the legs and one wing, and set him up on a bench on his chest and neck, with the vent sticking up facing the other worker, who masturbated the turkey's vent until it opened up and the white semen oozed forth. Using a vacuum pump, he sucked it into a syringe. Then Mason would catch another tom, and the same thing would happen again and again until the syringe was filled with semen.

Workers in the hen house had a harder task. Mason described it like this:

The hens weigh 20 to 30 pounds and are terrified, beating their wings and struggling in panic. They go through this every week for more than a year, and they don't like it. Once you have grabbed her with one hand, you flop her down chest first on the edge of the pit with the tail end sticking up. You put your free hand over the vent and tail and pull the rump and tail feathers upward. At the same time, you pull the hand holding the feet downward, thus "breaking" the hen so that her rear is straight up and her vent open. The inseminator sticks his thumb right under the vent and pushes, which opens it further until the end of the oviduct is exposed. Into this, he inserts a straw of semen connected to the end of a tube from an air compressor and pulls a trigger, releasing a shot of compressed air

> that blows the semen solution from the
> straw and into the hen's oviduct. Then
> you let go of the hen and she flops away.

In most jurisdictions, sexually assaulting
an animal is a crime. How does what Mason
depicts differ from a sexual assault on the
hen? I grant that the worker is not seeking
any kind of sexual satisfaction, but what
difference does that make to the hen? As
we saw earlier, wild turkey hens exercise
choice when they select which toms they
will allow to mate with them, preferring
those with longer snoods. "While males
may strut with abandon, females ultimately
choose their mates," Anne Readel, a biolo-
gist and wildlife photographer has written.
No wonder the hens don't like it! They have
no choice about who touches a sensitive
area of their anatomy—one that they do not

allow males with shorter snoods to get to. Moreover, as Mason points out, the workers are under pressure to get this done quickly:

Routinely, methodically, the breakers and the inseminator did this over and over, bird by bird, 600 toms per hour, or ten a minute. Each breaker "breaks" five hens a minute, or one hen every 12 seconds, 300 an hour, ten hours a day. At this speed, the handling of birds has to be fast and rough. It was the hardest, fastest, dirtiest, most disgusting, worst-paid work I have ever done. For ten hours we grabbed and wrestled birds, jerking them upside down, facing their pushed-open assholes, dodging their spurting shit, while breathing air filled with dust and feathers stirred up by panicked birds. Through all that, I received a torrent of

> verbal abuse from the foreman and oth-
> ers on the crew. I lasted one day.

In a competitive marketplace, saving on labor costs, even on the most poorly paid jobs, increases profits. Hence the pressure to work as fast as possible and the abuse from the foreperson when a worker can't do it quickly enough. It's bad for the workers and worse still for the animals, who cannot complain about what the abused and pressured workers are doing to them.

This is what the National Turkey Federation says about how artificial insemination affects the hen:

> To maintain production continuity, lay-
> ing hens are artificially inseminated in
> a controlled environment. During a 25-
> week laying cycle, a hen normally lays

80–100 eggs. At the end of this cycle, the hen is "spent" and usually processed.

The first sentence, which implies that without artificial insemination, there would be some interruptions in production, is deliberately misleading. Everyone in the industry knows that artificial insemination is not "to maintain production continuity" but rather to allow the turkey industry to produce birds with a body shape so distorted that they cannot mate. Without artificial insemination, the production of the breed most favored by producers and consumers would cease altogether. The second sentence tells us that for nearly six months, female turkeys are repeatedly raped and forced to lay a huge number of eggs. The final sentence tells us that the producers, after putting their birds through this ordeal, regard them as "spent." The birds could still live for several years, but they are spent in the sense that their bodies are exhausted by laying so many eggs in a short time and so the rate at which they lay fertile eggs is declining. That means they no longer have any commercial value. Nothing could better display the callousness of turkey producers than that heartless word "spent." That is why they are then "processed"—that is, trucked to the slaughterhouse and killed. Obviously, the idea of letting the birds out on a pasture to recover from their ordeal doesn't enter the minds of industrial turkey producers. It wouldn't pay.

*

Now that you know how most US turkeys are conceived, you also have a way to fill those awkward silences that can occur around the Thanksgiving table. Just ask the family and friends gathered together if they know how the bird they are eating was conceived. If they don't, enlighten them. Then ask them whether ensuring that everyone can get a generous slice of turkey breast is worth breeding a misshapen bird who cannot mate, requiring poorly paid workers to spend all day masturbating male turkeys and pushing open the vaginas of female turkeys, who hate the procedure, but have no escape from it until they are sent off to be killed.

Chapter 4

How They Live

Fertilized eggs are sent to hatcheries, where the young turkeys hatch out of their eggs. Then they are prepared for life in intensive confinement because that is where 998 of every 1,000 turkeys raised in the United States spend their lives. According to the 2022 Census of Agriculture, compiled by the US Department of Agriculture (USDA), of the more than 257 million turkeys produced in the United States in that year, approximately 230 million were raised in facilities that produced 60,000 or more turkeys. Only 317,356—not much more than 1 in 1,000— were raised in facilities that produced fewer than 2,000 turkeys, which by the standards of traditional family farms, is still a huge number of turkeys. In 1910, the average farm with turkeys had only 4 birds.

The USDA often uses the term "farm" to refer to places where tens of thousands, hundreds of thousands, or even millions of animals are kept confined. The official title for them is Concentrated Animal Feeding Operations, or CAFOs, but a CAFO bears no resemblance to traditional farms in which animals are out in the fields. CAFOs are factories, typically owned by or contracted to giant agribusiness corporations in which billions of sentient beings (not only turkeys, but cows, pigs, chickens, ducks, and fish) play the role of machines, converting the cheap raw materials—typically corn and soybean meal, but for fish, mostly pellets made from other, low-value fish—into higher-priced meat, eggs, milk, or fish. The food the animals eat frequently has to be transported long distances, and the animals use most of its nutritional value just to keep their bodies warm and hearts pumping, move around, and develop parts of their bodies that we do not eat, like bones and some internal organs. The extent of this wastage varies from species to species, but for all of them, whether we are focused on calories or protein, from eating their flesh we get back less than one-third of the nutritional value of the feed we provide for them. No wonder that Frances Moore Lappe, in her 1971 book *Diet for a Small Planet*, called these facilities "a protein factory in reverse." Yet over the past 50 years, CAFOs have multiplied, increasing the demand for soy and grains as well as putting more pressure on forests, including the Amazon

Rainforest and others, which are being cleared to grow food for animals. This is not the way to reduce our greenhouse gas emissions, nor to protect biodiversity or feed a growing world population.

Mutilations

How, then, do hatcheries prepare the young turkeys for life in a turkey factory? In discussing the cognitive abilities of turkeys, we saw that they will, if given the opportunity, form a social group of about 20 individuals in which all the birds know their place in the hierarchy. But turkeys destined for commercial production today are more likely to be with 10,000 or more other birds. The crowding leads to fighting and pecking, with dominant turkeys often inflicting severe injuries on the weaker birds.

In addition to the sheer number of turkeys crowded together, another factor in causing the aggression may be that in the absence of normal foraging activities, turkeys are bored and frustrated. According to one observer, young wild turkeys spend 86 to 95 percent of the day foraging. Young turkeys in intensive confinement have no opportunity to forage.

When turkeys lose feathers, often from being pecked at or having feathers pulled by other birds, they will show exposed skin or wounds, and this is likely to become a target for more pecking. Other birds may then join in, until they kill and eat the weaker bird. An outbreak of cannibalism can quickly become costly for the producer. To eliminate the cause of this behavior, the producer would have to allow turkeys foraging opportunities and the chance to live in groups of a size that they can handle, thus reducing their stress and the resulting aggression. Alternatively, the producer could select from genetic strains of birds who are less prone to aggression. Providing the conditions in which turkeys can forage and live in small groups, however, would increase costs, as would using birds who are less aggressive, but gain weight more slowly. So for the producers, it makes economic sense to accept some losses from cannibalism rather than to give the turkeys the conditions in which cannibalism would not occur.

Hence the standard approach is not to reduce stress or aggression in the birds but instead to reduce the losses by curtailing their ability to inflict damage on each other. That means cutting off the point of each bird's beak and partially amputating their toes to remove the sharp ends.

Removing the end of the beak of a turkey or chicken used to be known in the poultry industry as "debeaking," but in the interests of better public relations, it is now referred to as "beak trimming." If that term suggests that it is a simple and painless procedure, like trimming your fingernails, then once again, the industry has misled you. Here is what the USDA's Extension Services says:

> The beak of most poultry species is a very specialized organ. It contains many sensory receptors and glands that help the animal engage in activities such as searching for food and preening feathers. . . . The tissue between the bone and the outer horny layer contains many nerves.

Beak trimming is often performed by grabbing the fully conscious young birds and shoving their beaks into a device that uses a hot blade to cut through the beak and nerve tissue, then cauterize it. These operators are, like artificial inseminators, under pressure to do this as quickly as possible. Infrared light is now also used to damage the beak so that within a week or two, the tip falls off. Both methods involve acute pain to the birds, and no pain relief is provided. The birds lose sensory function in the beak too. Sometimes the severed nerves develop into neuromas—tumors of nerve tissue—which may cause pain for the remainder of the birds' lives.

Young turkeys undergo partial toe amputation in the belief that this will reduce the number of carcasses with scratches. Like beak trimming, this is a painful procedure, performed without anesthesia or pain relief. In a randomized controlled trial conducted by Canadian poultry researchers, turkeys who had their toes trimmed spent more time over the five days after the trimming both sitting and resting, and less time walking and feeding, than turkeys whose toes were not trimmed. The researchers regarded the reduced time spent feeding in birds genetically selected to have immense appetites as "a strong indicator of pain." Even as late as the 133rd day after the procedure—just one week before the turkeys were killed—the researchers found behavioral data indicative of reduced welfare in the turkeys who had undergone partial toe amputation. Neuromas have also been documented following toe amputation in chickens, where they persisted throughout the 60-day observation period. Yet in another study, the same research team found that the amputations had no positive effect on carcass quality and negative effects on body weight, making one wonder why they have been happening for all of these years.

Turkeys may also be mutilated in other ways: their snoods may be removed because the bright red flesh may attract pecking from other birds; sometimes the long claw or spur on the back of the leg is amputated; and the wing feathers may be trimmed to prevent the birds from flying and so decreasing flightiness in the flock. I have been unable to find research on how painful these procedures are and what impact they may have on the birds' welfare.

Confinement

After the hatchery mutilates the young turkeys, they are sorted into males and females so that the sexes can be reared separately.

That's because male and female turkeys grow to different sizes and are slaughtered at different ages. It's much simpler to send an entire batch off to slaughter than to try to separate the males and females when there are thousands of birds together in a shed.

Then the turkeys are sent to the intensive confinement facility where they will spend the rest of their lives until they are transported to slaughter, usually in about 11 weeks for the hens and 16 to 18 weeks for the toms.

In 2023, an investigator for the animal advocacy organization Mercy for Animals obtained work on two intensive confinement facilities in Minnesota, where she took videos and kept a diary. On the day that a new batch of young turkeys arrived at the facility, her diary reads, "Around 38,000 baby turkeys, no more than 24 hours old, arrived today, looking lost." They were, of course, lacking the mothers' care that both wild and traditional farmyard turkeys would normally have—sheltering under her wings when they are newly hatched and then starting to explore their surroundings, but always under their mother's watchful eye, ensuring that they stay together with their siblings. In intensive confinement, initially, the infant turkeys are placed in a brooding area where they can keep warm under lights, and more easily find food and water—a poor substitute for a mother's loving attention. The video shows them in numbers that make it impossible for the investigator or anyone else to pay them individual attention.

By the third week, the investigator's video shows the turkeys in an enormous windowless shed with artificial light and ventilation. Their stubby beaks with the tips seared off and amputated toes are visible. In week 4, the investigator comments on one young bird shown in the video:

> Today I saw one of the "runts." She was silently opening and shutting her mouth, looking like she was gasping for breath and shaking her head over and over again. She kept walking to the other birds and attempting to bury her head in their feathers. My heart broke watching her.

Some of the most shocking scenes from the video come from week 5, in which a device known as a "poultry trainer" is turned on. It passes a 120-volt live electric current through wires above the turkeys' feed and water lines to prevent the birds from

perching on them. The investigator hears
birds yelping as they receive electric shocks.
Some of them get their feet and heads tan-
gled in the wires and are electrocuted. The
investigator can get to some of them in time
and untangle them, but there are far too
many birds for her to assist them all.

The standard stocking density for turkeys in the United States is 2 square feet
per hen and 3 square feet for the toms.
At first there seems to be plenty of space,
but as the video reveals, they keep running
into each when they try to carry out normal behaviors like dust bathing, flying, or
even getting water. As the birds grow, they
will fill the available space until the floor of
the shed is covered in turkeys, barely able
to move without bumping into or stepping
on each other. The shed is barren except
for the pipes providing water and food.

Although wild turkeys flutter up into trees to roost every evening, there are no perches or other raised areas in the turkey sheds, save for the feed and water lines that, as we have seen, the birds are prevented from getting onto.

If you enter the shed, the first thing that will hit you is a burning sensation in your eyes and throat, as they react to the ammonia in the air, which in turn comes from the droppings of thousands of birds, accumulated for up to a year in the sawdust or wood shavings that cover the floor. Although each batch of birds is sent to slaughter after about 3 to 4 months, in the United States, unless there is an outbreak of disease, sheds are typically only cleaned out once a year.

The ammonia makes visiting the shed unpleasant, and so workers spend as little time in it as possible. But they do get to breathe fresh air again when their tasks are done, unlike the turkeys, who will never do that until the day they are taken out to be slaughtered.

As we have seen, turkeys have been bred to put on weight quickly, and at slaughter, the average turkey today weighs almost twice as much as turkeys did in 1960. The contrast with the rate of growth of wild turkeys is even greater. At four months old, a male wild turkey will weigh no more than 8 pounds, whereas at the same age, a male turkey selectively bred for meat will weigh 41 pounds. That puts an enormous strain on their immature leg bones. Professor John Webster, a veterinarian and expert on the welfare of farmed animals, has studied a similar problem in fast-growing chickens and concluded that they are in pain for the last third of their lives—a situation that has been compared with forcing someone with arthritis in their legs to stand up all day long. Turkeys have even more leg problems than chickens because they are also bred to grow rapidly, but in addition, they are almost all broad-breasted whites, and birds of this breed have been described as "physiologically unbalanced." They walk or stand less than older breeds, presumably because it is painful for them to put weight on their legs. A study of turkeys at thirteen different slaughterhouses found that 60 percent had swelling of the foot pad and 41 percent had severe foot pad dermatitis, while 25 percent had arthritis. All of these birds are likely to have experienced pain when walking or standing. Once again, these problems could be avoided by genetic selection of the turkeys to be reared—in this case, selecting for slower growth to

give the birds' legs time to mature sufficiently to bear the weight of their bodies.
But the attitude of the industry to such a
suggestion was made clear by Scott Beyer,
poultry specialist at Kansas State University, when he wrote, "Although a small
percentage of birds may be predisposed
to leg problems, use of highly selected
fast-growing strains is recommended because savings in feed costs and time far
outweigh the loss of a few birds." Econom-
ics overrides the suffering of the turkeys,
every time. When Beyer refers to "the loss
of a few birds," he means the birds whose
condition is so bad that they die before
they are ready to be sent to slaughter at 3
or 4 months of age. Remember that those
deaths are occurring in birds of a species
that, when not bred for maximum breast
meat, could live for ten years. Nor are these

deaths so "few" except relative to the 210 million turkeys raised and slaughtered in the United States. According to the "US Poultry Industry Manual," "[Turkey] hens usually finish with total mortality of 5–6% while total tom mortality is 10–12%," and according to the USDA, 57 percent of turkeys slaughtered are toms and 43 percent hens. Let's do the calculations on those numbers, conservatively taking the low end of the mortality range. Then we find that in 2022, producers started out with 133 million toms and sent 119.7 million to slaughter, whereas with hens, the figures are 95.1 million hatched and 90.3 million sent to slaughter. Putting both sexes together tells us that when Beyer dismisses the loss of a few birds, he is saying that the savings in feed costs and time outweigh the painful deaths of 18 million young birds.

In addition to the leg and foot problems suffered by many turkeys, the study of turkeys at 13 slaughterhouses found that 30 percent of them had blisters or other sores on the skin around their breastbone. These "breast buttons," as they are called, commonly occur in turkeys who spend most of their time lying down on their sternum. One factor in causing these sores may be the bird droppings in the litter of sawdust or wood shavings that covers the shed floor. The droppings are alkaline, and when there is moisture in the litter or on the bird's skin, it can cause a caustic burn on the part of the bird that is pressed into it. So for these deliberately deformed turkeys, there is no escape from pain. If they lie down to avoid the pain of carrying their heavy, unbalanced bodies on their arthritic legs and swollen feet, they end up with painful sores on their breastbone.

The Mercy for Animals undercover video shows turkeys at week 15, some of whom have obviously been victims of aggression from other turkeys. They have extensive bloody wounds in their necks, cracked scalps, or are bleeding from their eyes. The investigator reported some of these problems to the manager, who took no action. There are too many turkeys for anyone to bother about the suffering of individuals.

The Parents

This is what life is like for the birds whose bodies are on the table at Thanksgiving. Let's now consider the parents of those turkeys. We have already seen that they must either be masturbated for semen or forcibly inseminated, but that is not the only problem they face. The parents, known in the industry as breeders, must have the genes that give rise to the traits the producers want in their offspring: a prodigious appetite and a tendency to grow very quickly. Yet they need to live longer than the birds raised for meat, because to produce eggs or semen they need to reach sexual maturity, and of course, having raised them to maturity, the producers want them to perform their function for close to six months. Here is the problem: if the breeders are fed as much as they want, they will, over their longer lives, grow even more obese than their shorter-lived offspring, develop even more severe skeletal abnormalities, and cheat their producers by dying from heart disease or organ failure before they have produced enough semen or eggs to pay for the cost of rearing them. Producers overcome this problem by giving the parent birds only half as much food as they would eat if they could. This practice is also used with parent birds in the chicken industry, and behavioral studies there have shown that birds restricted to half-rations are chronically hungry and search in vain for food. It is unlikely to be any different for the parent turkeys.

Chapter 5

How They Die

When the turkeys in a shed reach market weight, their food is abruptly cut off to reduce "gastrointestinal splatter"—that is, to prevent the contents of the bird's intestines from splattering over and contaminating the rest of the carcass after the bird has been killed. For these birds, accustomed to having food readily available and bred to want to eat constantly, the sudden complete absence of food must cause great distress. But much worse is to come. A 2012 Mercy for Animals undercover video taken at Butterball turkey facilities in North Carolina shows workers moving turkeys out of a shed, repeatedly kicking the ones who are not moving fast enough, or picking them up and hurling them into crates on the back of a truck. Sometimes the birds are herded onto a conveyor belt that dumps them into the crates, which may spare them some broken bones, but must still be a terrifying experience for birds who have known only the inside of the shed. Depending on the distance to the slaughterhouse, transport and slaughter may take up to 18 hours, with the birds exposed to extremes of heat and cold, and now without access to water as well as food. Legally, the journey could take even longer because in the United States, the federal legislation regulating when animals must be given food and water on long journeys does not cover turkeys, chickens, or ducks. The only real constraint on the length of the journey is the number of turkeys who will die if it is any longer. As it is, each year, hundreds of thousands of turkeys die from the stress of the journey before they arrive at the slaughterhouse.

They may be the lucky ones. For the survivors, the next ordeal is being removed from the shipping crates, turned upside down, and having their legs rammed into metal shackles, sometimes with such force that the legs are broken. The shackles, with the turkeys hanging from them, move along a conveyor belt. The belt is supposed to dip the birds' heads into an electrified water bath that stuns them before they have their throats cut. But some birds pull their heads up when they pass the water bath and are still fully conscious when their throats are cut. Even when birds are in contact with the electrified water, because of concerns that too strong a current can damage the quality of the flesh, the current may be insufficient to induce unconsciousness. A study of 8 commercial slaughterhouses in France and Spain found signs of consciousness in significant numbers of turkeys at the time when they were having their throats cut, although the slaughterhouses were using a water bath stunner. European law requires the humane stunning of all birds and mammals prior to slaughter, whereas the US Humane Methods of Slaughter Act mentions cows, pigs, horses, mules, and sheep, but not chickens, turkeys, or any other birds. Hence in the United States, there is no legal requirement for slaughterhouses to stun turkeys before cutting their throats and letting them bleed to death, which makes it unlikely that US slaughterhouses do a better job of stunning turkeys than European ones.

Then there is the human factor. The people whose task it is to unload the turkeys from the shipping crates and place their feet into the shackles are expected to work all day long, once again under pressure to keep up with the speed of the slaughter line, and in physically unpleasant as well as psychologically and emotionally difficult conditions for low pay and even lower status. Often they don't last long; in some plants, the annual staff turnover is above 100 percent, meaning that the average worker doesn't even last one year in the job. It isn't surprising that these workers sometimes vent their anger and frustration on the only beings who are lower than they are: the turkeys they are unloading. That's why, again and again, undercover investigations of slaughterhouses reveal shocking abuse of animals.

People for the Ethical Treatment of Animals (PETA) and Mercy for Animals have both sent undercover investigators to

slaughterhouses that kill turkeys for Butterball, which markets its turkeys as "the
highest quality product" and boasts that
its products have been certified humane
by the American Humane Association. (If
that is true, it is greatly to the discredit of
the American Humane Association, which
should not be confused with either the Humane Society of the United States or the
Humane League.) At a plant that shackles
and kills about 50,000 birds every day, the
PETA investigator saw a worker trying to
get a turkey out of a crate when its foot was
stuck in the crate's wire. The worker simply ripped the turkey's foot off its body. The
terrified birds flap their wings and try to
escape when the workers grab them. The
investigator recorded one worker saying
to another, "When they start doing that,
when they struggle, hit them up against the

shackle, or hit them up against the trailer."
The investigator videoed the worker doing
that, and another worker punching a turkey. A worker is heard boasting, "I kicked
the fuck out of the motherfucker." Sometimes, birds get loose and run under the
truck's tires. The workers were instructed
not to go under the trucks, and the investigator could hear popping sounds when the
truck moved forward. Once the truck had
left, there were squashed remains of birds
where it had been. We've seen this before:
individual birds do not count. To take the
time to save them just doesn't pay.

"Depopulation"

The methods used to kill turkeys in US
slaughterhouses are often grossly inhu-
mane, but there is one kind of death, inflicted

on millions of turkeys, that is even worse. This method of killing is done when bird flu—officially, Highly Pathogenic Avian Influenza, or HPAI—is detected in at least one bird on premises where turkeys are kept. Even if only a few birds test positive, to prevent the virus spreading, all the turkeys on the premises are killed.

The method of killing that is worse than US slaughterhouses is known in the industry as Ventilation Shutdown Plus, usually abbreviated to VSD+. It is being used to kill chickens, ducks, turkeys, and pigs by the thousands or even hundreds of thousands at a time. Briefly, a shed full of animals, or sometimes one section of a shed into which the animals are concentrated, is made as airtight as possible by blocking exhaust fans that allow air to get in or out. Heaters are brought into the shed. The ventilation system is turned off, and the heaters are turned on.

Our Honor, an organization of veterinarians opposed to this method of killing animals, has obtained, by requesting state records, official reports of some of these killings. The documents include the guidelines for depopulation by VSD+, which require that the temperature in the shed must reach between 104°F and 110°F within 30 minutes and should not fall below that temperature for at least 3 hours.

Each of the reports obtained by Our Honor describes a particular "depopulation" of many birds, usually a shed full, although the actual number killed is blacked out. The reports for turkeys record how long it took for 50 percent of the turkeys to die and how long for 100 percent to die. To give one example, similar to many others:

in Meeker County, Minnesota, on October 9, 2023, a shed of turkeys was "depopulated." The report form was completed by a veterinarian whose name appears at the bottom of the form, but because the problem is far larger than any individual, I will not publish the individual's name. Instead, I will mention that the turkeys were being produced for Jennie-O Turkey Store, the provider of the turkeys absurdly "pardoned" by President Biden the following month. Under "Setup and Preparation Activities," the veterinarian has written, "Emptied feed pans and raised [in other words, removed] water and feed lines in barn. Two flocks in barn. Both flocks penned to the east end of the barn. Any holes or gaps in the curtain sealed with plastic. Plastic to seal middle divider of barn." The "Primary Depopulation Method" is described as "Ventilation

Shutdown + heat" and recorded as having started at 9:28 a.m. The "Approximate time at 50% mortality" was 11:00 a.m., and the "time at 100% mortality or cessation of primary method" was 12:45 p.m. Below that is a section headed "Secondary Depopulation Method: Captive Bolt Gun." A note added here reads, "Turkeys that were unable to be moved to the east end. Most leg injuries." For this section, the "finish time (100% mortality)" is given as 9:00 a.m. In other words, the turkeys with leg injuries who could not be moved to the east end of the barn were killed first and would have had a far quicker death because they were killed using a handgun that fires a bolt into the head of the animal. (The bolt remains attached to the gun, hence "captive bolt.") But this method was not used for the other turkeys, presumably because there were thousands of them, and it would

have been more expensive and taken longer
to employ the workers needed to kill the turkeys individually.

The industry calls this, euphemistically,
"depopulation," and when it is reported in
the media, the birds are often described as
being "euthanized"—although being heated
to death is anything but the "good death"
that is the meaning of the Greek words
from which "euthanasia" was formed. The
turkeys, unable even to obtain water, will
try desperately to escape the heat before
they die from heatstroke. Moreover, in 51
percent of turkey houses in which VSD+
was used, the method did not even kill all
the birds. Some had to be killed after they
survived the heat. USDA reports show that
when a secondary method, such as a captive
bolt pistol, was needed to kill birds who survived heatstroke, the survivors were often

left to suffer the impact of heatstroke on their bodies until the next day, when someone would put them out of their misery.

USDA records obtained by the Animal Welfare Institute under the Freedom of Information Act make it possible to calculate that from February 2022 to December 2023, at least 13.4 million turkeys died or were "depopulated" in the HPAI pandemic that swept the United States. Roughly 2.1 million turkeys were killed on premises on which VSD+ was the only method used, and about 4.7 million were killed on premises on which both VSD+ and other methods were used. Far larger numbers of chickens have been killed by VSD+, and it has also been used on at least 243,016 pigs.

There are less cruel methods of killing large numbers of intensively confined animals. Studies published as long ago as 2010 showed that filling the sheds with foam containing nitrogen gas caused a rapid loss of consciousness and cessation of movement within about 60 seconds. That is still not ideal, but it is far better than succumbing after 3 hours of extreme heat. In the European Union and United Kingdom, nitrogen is used when it is necessary to kill animals rapidly and in large numbers. When nitrogen is pumped into a shed in the form of high-expansion foam consisting of nitrogen-filled bubbles, movement ceases rapidly, and the animals appear to die without prolonged distress. The American Association of Swine Veterinarians classifies the use of foam bubbles filled with nitrogen as a "preferred" method of mass killing for pigs. It is also clearly less cruel than VSD+ for chickens, ducks, and turkeys.

Why, then, aren't more humane methods widely used in the United States? At least since 2014, when the previous major outbreak of HPAI occurred in the United States, it has been predictable that there would be further outbreaks. That's because during that outbreak, the virus spread from sheds crowded with chickens and turkeys to wild birds, who now act as a reservoir for the virus, even when the harshest measures are taken to control it in commercially raised birds. (The transmission of HPAI from factory farms to wild birds is, of course, a disaster for biodiversity as well.) The chicken and turkey industries had ample time to plan for and obtain the resources to deal with the next outbreak of HPAI in a manner that killed birds far less cruelly than VSD+. One reason they did not do so seems to have been that in the United States, there is no legal requirement or public pressure to find a solution that causes less suffering. In the European Union and the United Kingdom, the attitude of the public as well as the laws and regulations are much less tolerant of cruelty to animals.

The American Veterinary Medical Association (AVMA) bears significant responsibility for the widespread and continuing use of VSD+ in the United States. In the current (2019) edition of its *Guidelines for the Depopulation of Animals*, the AVMA lists VSD+ as "permitted in constrained circumstances." Crucially, the AVMA's stance on VSD+ is at odds with the World Organization for Animal Health, the leading global body concerned with animal health and welfare, and with veterinary and other expert scientific opinion all over the world. Killing animals by VSD+ is not accepted in Australia, the European Union, or United Kingdom. The European Food Safety Authority, an official body of the European Union, has published documents on the welfare of both pigs and poultry when they are killed for purposes other than slaughter. The document on pigs lists killing methods that are likely to be "highly painful" and "must never be used." The list includes, along with burying alive and drowning: "ventilation shutdown with or without additional provision of heat or CO_2." The document on poultry, which includes turkeys, states that "ventilation shutdown should not be used as a killing method," and even warns that when using gas to kill the birds, "prolonged periods of ventilation shutdown" should be avoided before the gas is injected because that "can lead to heat stress."

Dr. Crystal Heath, a veterinarian and the founder of Our Honor, has said that the AMVA's acceptance of VSD+ is a violation of the basic ethical precepts that should underpin veterinary practice and undermines the honor of the profession. Dr. Jim Reynolds, a past chair of the AVMA Animal Welfare Committee and a professor of large animal medicine and welfare at Western University College of Veterinary Medicine in Pomona, California, says that the use of VSD+ "violates the veterinary oath and must be prohibited." Professor Barry Kipperman, who teaches veterinary ethics at both the University of California, Davis, School of Veterinary Medicine and the University of Missouri, describes the AVMA's sanctioning of VSD+ as "a betrayal" of everything that the veterinary profession stands for because it places "human expediency" above

animal welfare. Dr. George Bates, an emeritus professor of veterinary medical tech-
nology at Wilson College and a member of
the AVMA for more than 50 years, consid-
ers that farmed animal veterinarians, who
make up a small fraction of the total AVMA
membership, exert a "wildly disproportion-
ate" influence on AVMA policies pertaining
to agricultural animals. As he puts it, they
"take on the outlook of their corporate pay-
masters, abandon ethical principles, adopt
a strictly mercantile attitude towards their
purported patients, and fully embrace the
profit-driven ethos of Big Ag."

The AVMA's recommendations are de-
cisive because the USDA takes its rules for
killing farmed animals directly from the
AVMA's *Guidelines*. In the case of animals
killed to prevent the spread of disease such
as HPAI, this affects the eligibility of the

industrial animal producers to receive financial compensation from the USDA for the value of the animals they have killed.

Now that I have described VSD+ and mentioned financial compensation, it's time to make good on my promise in chapter 1 to explain how Jennie-O Turkey Store, the provider of the turkeys pardoned by President Biden before Thanksgiving 2023, the country's largest turkey producer and a subsidiary of the even more gigantic Hormel Foods Corporation, received nearly $106 million for heating animals to death. To be precise, official USDA records show that between February 2022 and April 2024, Jennie-O received federal government payments of $105,855,157 to compensate it for the turkeys it had "depopulated," many of them by VSD+. Many other turkey producers received millions as well. Tyson

Foods, one of the world's largest meat producers, received $29,709,942. Butterball, the country's second-largest turkey producer, received the comparatively modest sum of $6,311,715.

Effectively, the federal government is providing free insurance to US agribusiness corporations against the financial risk involved in intensively producing chickens and turkeys in an era of HPAI. If you are a US taxpayer, that's your taxes going to yet another subsidy for businesses that provide poor conditions for their workers, are wasteful of food and disastrous for the environment, and inflict a vast universe of suffering on animals.

Chapter 6

Reconsider the Turkey

In my books *Animal Liberation* and *Animal
Liberation Now*, I argued that we should give
as much consideration to the suffering of
a nonhuman animal as we give to a similar
amount of human suffering. Of course, different kinds of animals will have different
capacities for suffering, and that is often
relevant to how much a being is suffering,
but what matters is how much the being
suffers, not what species the being is.

That principle also holds when we com-
pare the suffering of two animals, one a
member of a species many of us have as
companion animals and have come to love,

such as a dog or budgerigar, and the other a member of a species few of us love and many of us eat, like a pig or turkey. Recall Cornelius, the "handsome, outgoing, and intelligent" turkey who was lucky enough to be taken in by Steve and Derek, who do not divide animals into two distinct categories, those to be petted and those to be eaten. They had no difficulty in seeing Cornelius the turkey and Esther the pig as individuals with wants and needs, just as those who live with dogs and cats see their companion animals. And what is true of Cornelius and Esther is true of pigs and turkeys in general: they are all individuals, with their own personalities as well as their own capacities to experience pain and pleasure. To raise them in conditions dominated by the drive to cut costs, in which their individual experiences count for nothing, is indefensible.

To give less weight to the sufferings of sentient beings simply because of their species is "speciesism," a term coined by British animal advocate Richard Ryder. In the nearly fifty years since I argued against speciesism in *Animal Liberation*, the literature on the ethics of our treatment of animals has boomed. Some of these books and articles have sought to defend speciesism, but I do not think any of them have succeeded. On the contrary, philosophers working in distinct ethical traditions are now converging on the view that our current treatment of animals is a grave moral wrong.

I take the utilitarian view that the right action is the one that does the most to reduce pain and suffering, and increase pleasure and happiness, for all beings capable of having those experiences—in other words, for all sentient beings. Philosophers who base their views on the idea that individuals have inherent rights disagree with utilitarians on some issues, but many of them accept that, as Tom Regan argued, animals have rights that are routinely violated in today's production of meat, eggs, and dairy products. Christine Korsgaard, perhaps the world's most prominent Kantian ethicist, regards animals as our "fellow creatures" and thinks that Immanuel Kant himself was mistaken to say that because they lack self-consciousness, they may, in contrast to humans, be treated as means rather than as ends in themselves. Martha Nussbaum draws on the thought of Aristotle, who believed that animals exist in order to provide humans with food and leather, but Nussbaum rejects that view, as any post-Darwinian thinker must, and holds that justice requires allowing beings to flourish in accordance with their capabilities, which makes our industrial animal production a glaring example of injustice. Nor are such objections to our treatment of animals confined to secular philosophers. Christians like Andrew Linzey, David Clough, and Charles Camosy reach similar conclusions on Christian grounds, while in a dialogue I had with a leading Buddhist thinker, Shih Chao-Hwei, we found ourselves closely aligned on the importance of encouraging people to avoid eating animals.

Nevertheless, for the purpose of this book, I do not need to go so far as to argue that it is wrong to give more weight to the suffering of a human being than we give to a similar amount of suffering experienced by a nonhuman animal. Instead, I ask you to imagine that you learn that in the country in which you live and vote, hundreds of millions of dogs are being raised for food, and that this enormous industry treats all of these dogs, from conception to slaughter, or when they are infected with "Highly Pathogenic Canine Influenza," in the same way that the turkey industry in the United States now treats turkeys.

What would you think of such an industry? Would you support it by purchasing its products? Or would you support organizations working to abolish it, and vote for politicians who pledged to do so? Would you participate in a festive meal in which the carcass of one of these dogs, suitably roasted, was carved up and eaten?

If, as I hope and expect, you would be appalled by such an industry, would boycott its products, would vote for politicians who pledged to abolish it, and would never, ever sit around a table at which the carcass of one of these dogs was carved up and eaten, then you should not act any differently with regard to the existing US turkey industry. Turkeys and dogs are not the same, but they are both capable of living enjoyable and relatively pain-free lives for several years. The differences between them cannot justify us being horrified at an industry that would treat dogs as we now treat turkeys, while we support, with our purchases and consumption, an industry that treats turkeys as our existing turkey industry does.

What, then, will you eat at whatever holiday feast you celebrate? The simplest option is to ditch the animal centerpiece, but keep all the trimmings, which for many people is the best part of the meal anyway. For Thanksgiving, some buy a tofu-based "turkey" or concoct their own turkey-like centerpiece from tofu or seitan, which can go well with cranberry sauce. If you are so rigidly traditionalist that you absolutely must eat turkey at your feast, the least you can do is to plan ahead and order one of the few slow-growing, heritage breed, pasture-raised turkeys available. Try to find one that is killed on the farm rather than being trucked to a slaughterhouse, and of course, expect to pay much more for it. Your bird will at least have missed out on a great deal of the suffering endured by misshapen and intensively confined broad-breasted whites, and if you can find a producer who keeps their turkeys in small groups with ample outdoor space, and allows the mother to hatch and then take care of her young, your turkey may even have had a good, though short life.

Recipes for Ethical Feasting

Every year since I came to the United States in 1999, I have joined a group of friends for Thanksgiving. None of us eat meat, and each of us brings something to the feast. Here are a few recipes we have enjoyed that I hope will become part of a new "traditional" holiday feast for you and your friends and family.

Main Course

Since I wrote this book to persuade you to reconsider the turkey, let's start with that. Philosopher Karen Bennett brings a seitan "turkey." Seitan is the Japanese name for a traditional high-protein food that is also used in East and Southeast Asia, and often served in Buddhist restaurants—for example, as mock duck. It is made from the protein in wheat and can have a chewy, meatlike texture. Here's what Karen writes:

Seitan Turkey

A vegetarian or vegan holiday meal doesn't *require* a centerpiece protein, of course, but sometimes you want one. This holds its own on the Thanksgiving or any holiday table alongside stuffing, vegan gravy, and all the other sides. It's both festive and tasty. Further, it not only *can* be made a day ahead but also is better that way because the seitan firms up as it cools. You can fully cook it or pause after the step where you wrap it in raw pie crust.

DRY INGREDIENTS

2 cups gluten flour, sometimes called vital
   wheat gluten

½ cup soy or chickpea flour

½ cup nutritional yeast flakes

½ teaspoon salt

WET MIX

1 block firm tofu (12 oz), drained

1½ cups water

3 tablespoons soy sauce

1 tablespoon olive oil

½ yellow onion

3 cloves of garlic

COOKING LIQUID

About 8 cups homemade or store-bought
   vegetarian stock, preferably "chicken
   style." (You can add nutritional yeast to
   vegetarian stock to get a richer flavor.)

The Seitan

Preheat the oven to 325°F.

Mix the dry ingredients in a large bowl, preferably one that works with an electric mixer with a dough hook. Blend the wet mix in a blender or food processor. Pour the wet mix into the bowl with the dry ingredients and mix with the dough hook for about 10 minutes. Let it rest for 20 minutes or more, and knead with the dough hook for another 10 minutes. (If you don't have a dough hook, you'll have to knead it by hand. It is much heavier and denser than typical bread dough, so be prepared to get a workout.) Don't skimp on the kneading time; it is crucial for developing the gluten and thus the texture of the final product.

Remove the dough from the bowl. Cut off two smallish pieces to shape into cylinders for the drumsticks. Shape the rest into a mounded oblong, to be the body of the turkey. Don't stress about this; precision is not possible, and whatever you do will deform during cooking. You're just going for the rough idea.

Pour the broth into an oven-safe pot with a lid, like a "dutch oven." Place the 3 seitan pieces into the liquid, cover the pot, and put in the oven. Bake for roughly 3 hours, flipping the seitan over a few times starting about halfway through the cooking time. At about 3 hours, remove the lid, and if there is still liquid in the pot, bake for about 30 more minutes. The seitan will then feel spongy, not super firm, but nonetheless with a very different texture than when it was raw. Remove from the pot and let cool. When cool, trim to get closer to your desired shape. Meanwhile, make the "skin."

The Skin

The "skin" is simply pie crust. You can use any recipe you like as long as you follow two rules: if the recipe calls for sugar, leave it out, and make sure that it includes some salt (probably a ½ tsp); and make sure that the recipe makes enough for a top- and bottom-crusted pie or two open-faced pies.

Preheat the oven to the temperature your recipe calls for.

Roll the crust to ¼ inch thick. Refrigerate it for about 20 minutes.

Cut off about ¼ of it, and cut that in half again to yield two small pieces. Use those to wrap the "drumsticks," being sure to squeeze about one-third of the way along to yield a vaguely drumstick shape. Use the large remaining piece to wrap the main body of the seitan, keeping the seams underneath as far as possible. (*Now* you should aim for precision.) Slash the dough a few times across the top to release steam.

Line a baking pan with aluminum foil, arrange your sculpted "bird" to your liking, and bake until the crust is golden brown.

Garnish with sprigs of fresh sage and thyme, and perhaps scatter with pomegranate seeds.

This recipe is a modified and heavily rewritten version of one that used to be on http://vegan feastkitchen.blogspot.com, Bryanna Clark Grogan's website.

For those who want a gravy to go with their "turkey," one of our friends brings this mushroom gravy, following a recipe by Melissa Clark, published in the *New York Times*:

Vegan Mushroom Make-Ahead Gravy

INGREDIENTS

½ cup extra virgin olive oil

½ small onion, finely chopped (½ cup)

4 ounces baby portobello mushrooms,
   finely chopped (1 cup)

½ cup all-purpose flour

4 to 5 cups vegetable stock, preferably
   homemade, as needed

1 teaspoon soy sauce, or more to taste

½ teaspoon salt

¼ teaspoon black pepper

In a large skillet, heat oil over medium-high heat. Add onion and mushrooms; cook, stirring, until well browned, or about 8 to 10 minutes.

Sprinkle in flour and cook, stirring, until golden brown, or about 3 to 5 minutes.

Slowly whisk in vegetable stock, a little at a time, until a smooth sauce forms. Simmer 2 to 3 minutes until thickened. Season with soy sauce, salt, and pepper. Serve as is or pass it through a fine-mesh strainer.

This yields about 3½ cups.

Sides and Salads

Other friends bring various side dishes, like cranberry sauce, "stuffing"—not actually used to stuff anything, of course—and yams. Philosopher Dale Jamieson, who works on environmental ethics, climate change, and our treatment of animals, is an old friend. I met him at the first-ever conference on ethics and animals in 1978. It was Dale who introduced me to the other people attending our Thanksgiving dinners. He supplied these recipes for cranberry sauce and yams.

Cranberry Sauce

INGREDIENTS

12 ounces fresh organic cranberries

½ cup water

¼ cup + 3 tablespoons pure maple syrup

¼ cup fresh orange juice

½ teaspoon grated nutmeg

¼ teaspoon ground cinnamon

2 cinnamon sticks

Simmer the cranberries in boiling water, stir in the other ingredients, and set out at room temperature or chill before serving.

Maple Roasted Sweet Potato

INGREDIENTS

2 large sweet potatoes

¼ cup maple syrup

2 tablespoons brown sugar

¼ teaspoon cinnamon

2 tablespoons olive oil

Salt to taste

Bake at 400°F for 40 to 60 minutes.

Another philosopher, Michael Strevens, brings a refreshing beet salad. When I asked him for a recipe, Michael described it as a philosopher might: "more of an idea than a recipe." But he was eventually persuaded to write down his idea in a way that other people could follow:

Late Autumn Beet Salad

Take about 1 medium-sized beet per person, wrap in foil leaving an inch of greens attached, and roast at 400°F for about

75 minutes. (At 60 minutes, test the beets with a skewer to see whether they are cooked through.)

Peel the beets, cut into slices or cubes, and then toss with olive oil, balsamic vinegar, and salt and pepper, along with some mix of the following, almost equaling the beets in total quantity:

Sliced or cubed winter radishes (e.g., black radish or watermelon radish)
Sliced or cubed kohlrabi
Sliced or cubed green apple
Add ¼ pound or more of pea shoots just before serving and mix.
Another classic addition is ¼ cup of walnuts.

I'm a mushroom forager, and in the northeastern United States, October and early

November is the season for my favorite mushroom: hen of the woods. If you know what you are looking for, they are not difficult to find, and some are huge, weighing several pounds. They freeze well too, so I've always been able to bring enough to Thanksgiving to serve a few pieces to everyone as an appetizer. I cook them up just before serving.

Hen of the Woods

Slice your hen into pieces about as long as a finger, but they can be as wide as three fingers. Do your best to remove any dirt or grit. Hen of the woods is parasitic on deciduous trees, mostly oaks, and usually grows from a root or the base of the tree. If they grow entirely out of the aboveground part of the tree, they can be free of dirt or grit, but if they grow through soil, they will often have grit or dirt trapped in them. Although many people say you should never put mushrooms in water, using water to assist in the cleaning won't harm these mushrooms at all.

If you are freezing your hen, put the sliced and cleaned pieces in a plastic bag, tie it up, and put it in the freezer. Thaw before use. After thawing, squeeze out as much water as you can.

Heat a little olive oil in a large pan. Optionally, fry some sliced or crushed garlic in the oil. Add the hen pieces and sprinkle with a little soy sauce (don't overdo it or you will lose the excellent mushroom taste). When the mushroom pieces go brown and smell good, they are ready to serve.

We don't confine ourselves to traditional US Thanksgiving dishes. Chunmei Li, who works with Partners in Health and is Dale's wife, produces delicious dishes that come from China, the country of her birth, including this one:

Sichuan Tofu and Chinese Cabbage

INGREDIENTS

1 Chinese cabbage (also called Peking cabbage, napa cabbage, pe-tsai, and wombok), chopped in medium-sized pieces

1 pack of firm tofu, cut into 1-inch cubes

3 tablespoons oil

1 bunch bean thread noodles (also known as glass noodles)

2 tablespoons soy sauce

1 tablespoon Sichuan broad bean chili paste (doubanjiang); but if you don't want it spicy, you can substitute black

bean garlic sauce. What if you do like it spicy yet can't get Sichuan broad bean chili paste? You can try a different chili paste or mix some sriracha into the black bean garlic sauce.

2 fresh red or green chilies (choose the type of chili according to how spicy you want the dish)

3 cloves garlic, sliced or put through a garlic press

5 slices of ginger, finely chopped

1 scallion chopped into small pieces

1 tablespoon corn starch (optional)

Salt to taste

1. Heat the oil and toss the tofu cubes in it until golden. Put them aside.
2. Mix soy sauce with a little water in a bowl, and add the cornstarch and sriracha, if using.

3. Soak bean thread noodles in boiled water. When soft, cut them with kitchen scissors so that they are not too long.

4. Heat the oil and fry the garlic, ginger, and half of the fresh chili for 2 minutes over medium heat until fragrant, then add in either the Sichuan chili paste or black bean garlic sauce and fry another minute.

5. Add the chopped cabbage, bean thread noodles, and tofu.

6. Add the sauce mixture from step 2.

7. Cook over medium heat until the sauce mixture is boiling, then lower heat and simmer for about 6 minutes.

8. Garnish with scallions and the remaining fresh chili.

9. Add the cornstarch if you prefer a thicker sauce.

10. Add salt if needed.

Dessert

My wife, Renata, who at the moment is best described as a promoter of Yiddish cultural events, has made this wonderful vegan dessert. It is one of our favorites, and also a favorite of Lori Sandler, the founder of the vegan and nut-free Divvies Bakery in South Salem, New York.

Warm Apple-Apricot Cake

INGREDIENTS
Nonstick baking spray
3 cups flour
1 teaspoon salt
¾ teaspoon ground cinnamon
1 teaspoon baking soda
1 teaspoon baking powder
1½ cups canola oil

1½ cups sugar

½ cup applesauce (a 4-ounce snack pack
   contains about ½ cup)

⅓ cup apricot all-fruit spread (apricot jam)

3 cups ¼-inch-thick diced pieces of peeled,
   cored Granny Smith apples (about 5)

1. Preheat oven to 350°F.
2. Spray a bundt-style pan with a nonstick
   baking spray.
3. Whisk together the flour, salt, cinnamon, baking soda, and baking powder
   in a bowl and set aside.
4. (Renata uses a mixer from this point on.)
   In a separate bowl, whip together the oil
   and sugar with an electric mixer, increasing gradually to high speed, for a total of
   3 minutes. Add the applesauce and apricot spread, then mix on high speed for
   another minute until creamy.

5. Add the dry ingredients to the wet and mix on medium speed until well incorporated. Scrape down the sides of the bowl with a spatula and continue mixing. The batter will clump together.

6. Add the apples to the batter and mix on low speed until well combined. Pour the batter (which will be thick) into the prepared pan.

7. Bake in the oven for 60 to 70 minutes, rotating the pan halfway through. Test the center of the cake for doneness with a toothpick; the toothpick should come out clean. The cake may take a bit longer to bake if the apples are particularly juicy because the center will be extra moist. Turn the cake out of the pan onto a cooking rack immediately after removing from the oven.

Yield: 1 bundt cake; 12 slices.

Acknowledgments

This book began life as an essay published by Project Syndicate, for which I have been writing monthly essays for many years. It came to the attention of my editor at Princeton University Press, Rob Tempio, who proposed expanding it into a book, and I thank him for the suggestion as well as for guidance throughout the writing and editing of the text. Thanks also to his assistant, Chloe Coy; Karen Carter, who oversaw the production of the book; Cindy Milstein, who did the copyediting; the designer, Chris Ferrante; and my literary agent, Kathy Robbins, and Janet Oshiro at The Robbins Office for their helpful suggestions.

For the title of the original essay, and hence the book too, I am indebted to David Foster Wallace's fine essay "Consider the Lobster."

Sophie Kevany ably assisted with research, as she had previously done for *Animal Liberation Now*, and I am grateful to Open Philanthropy for a grant that enabled her to work on both books. As the text indicates, I have drawn on investigations conducted by Mercy for Animals and People for the Ethical Treatment of Animals.

I especially want to thank two veterinarians who are committed to putting the welfare of animals first: Crystal Heath, cofounder of Our Honor, and Gwendolen Reyes-Illg, who works for the Animal Welfare Institute. They have both been generous with their time in providing information and ensuring that the facts in this book are accurate, especially on the issue of "depopulation."

Notes on Sources

p. 2: Details of the origins of presidential turkey pardons are in "History of White House Thanksgiving Traditions," White House Historical Association, accessed March 5, 2024, https://www.whitehousehistory .org/press-room/press-backgrounders/history -of-white-house-thanksgiving-traditions. For the number of turkeys killed annually at Thanksgiving, see "Thanksgiving Turkey: How Many Turkeys Are Expected to Be Eaten This Year?," *Marca*, November 21, 2023, https://www.marca.com/en/lifestyle/us -news/2023/11/21/655ca99622601d286d8b4593 .html.

p. 5: The number of turkeys commercially produced in the United States in 2022 comes from "Raising America's Turkeys," National Turkey Federation, accessed March 5, 2024, https://www.eatturkey.org /raising-turkeys/.

p. 8: On the domestication of turkeys by Indigenous Americans, see A. W. Schorger, *The Wild Turkey: Its History and Domestication* (Norman: University of Oklahoma Press, 1966); Natalie D. Munro, "The Role of Turkey in the Southwest," in *Environment, Origins and Populations*, ed. William C. Sturtevant, vol. 3, *Handbook of North American Indians* (Washington, DC: Smithsonian Institution, 2006), 463–69. For evidence that female turkeys prefer males with longer snoods, see Richard Buchholz, "Mate Choice Research," University of Mississippi, Department of Biology, accessed March 5, 2024, https://biology .olemiss.edu/people/faculty/richard-buchholz /buchholz-mate-choice-research/.

p. 9: Fabian's description of Malvolio is in William Shakespeare, *Twelfth Night*, act II, scene 5. The myth that turkeys drown when it rains is debunked in Matthew Rozsa, "Stupid Turkeys? Scientists Say That the Unfairly Maligned Bird May Actually Be Stuffed with Smarts," Salon, November 25, 2021, https://www .salon.com/2021/11/25/turkeys-actually-smart/. On aggression among turkeys, especially when crowded indoors, see Jason G. Goldmann, "Nothing to Gobble At: Social Cognition in Turkeys," *Scientific American*, November 27, 2013, https://blogs.scientificamerican .com/thoughtful-animal/nothing-to-gobble-at -social-cognition-in-turkeys.

p. 12: That dogs can pass an olfactory mirror test is shown in Alexandra Horowitz, "Smelling Themselves: Dogs Investigate Their Own Odours Longer

When Modified in an 'Olfactory Mirror' Test," *Behavioural Processes* 143 (2017): 17–24. For the evidence that roosters recognize themselves in a mirror, see Sonja Hillemacher, Sebastian Ocklenburg, Onur Güntürkün, and Inga Tiemann, "Roosters Do Not Warn the Bird in the Mirror: The Cognitive Ecology of Mirror Self-Recognition," *PLoS ONE* 18, no. 10 (2023): e0291416, https://doi.org/10.1371/journal.pone.0291416.

p. 14: Information about Cornelius is drawn from Susan Cleland, "Life according to Cornelius," October 2, 2021, Happily Ever Esther Farm Sanctuary, https://www.happilyeveresther.ca/hog-blog/2021/10/2/life-according-to-cornelius. The figures on turkey production are provided in "Turkey by the Numbers," National Turkey Federation, accessed March 6, 2024, https://www.eatturkey.org/turkeystats/; "Turkey Sector: Background & Statistics," USDA, accessed March 6, 2024, https://www.ers.usda.gov/newsroom/trending-topics/turkey-sector-background-statistics/. The increasing weight of turkeys and the dominance of the broad-breasted white in US commercial turkey production are reported in Kenny Torella, "How America Broke the Turkey," *Vox*, November 22, 2023, https://www.vox.com/future-perfect/2023/11/22/23970874/thanksgiving-turkey-farming-jennie-o-hormel-white-house-pardon.

p. 17: The clinical description of the artificial insemination of a turkey is quoted in Keith Bramwell, "Artificial Insemination in Turkeys and Chickens," October 2022, *Merck Veterinary Manual*, https://www.msdvetmanual.com/poultry/artificial-insemination/artificial-insemination-in-turkeys-and-chickens.

p. 22: A version of Jim Mason's account of working as a turkey inseminator first appeared in Peter Singer and Jim Mason, *The Ethics of What We Eat* (New York: Rodale, 2006).

p. 22: The quote is from Anne Readel, "How Wild Turkeys Find Love," *New York Times*, November 21, 2022, https://www.nytimes.com/2022/11/21/travel/wild-turkeys-mates.html.

p. 25: The National Turkey Federation's false statement of the reason for artificial insemination can be found in "Raising America's Turkeys," accessed January 4, 2024, https://www.eatturkey.org/raising-turkeys/.

p. 29: The figure of 99.8 percent in intensive confinement comes from calculations made by Sentience Institute, https://www.sentienceinstitute.org/us-factory-farming-estimates. For the 2022 USDA Census of Agriculture, see https://www.nass.usda.gov/Publications/AgCensus/2022. For the 1910 figure of 4 turkeys per farm, see Colin G. Scanes, George Brant, and M. Eugene Ensminger, *Poultry Science*, 4th ed. (Old Bridge, NJ: Pearson Prentice Hall, 2004), 6.

p. 31: The original remark comes from Frances Moore Lappe and Joseph Collins, *Diet for a Small Planet* (New York: Ballantine Books, 1971). For a 2015 update, see "Meat Madness," Small Planet Institute, November 10, 2015, https://www.smallplanet.org/single-post/2016/11/10/meat-madness. On the increase in aggression when turkeys are crowded, see Joanna Marchewka, T. T. Watanabe, Valentina Ferrante, and Inma Estevez, "Review of the Social and Environmental Factors Affecting the Behavior and Welfare of Turkeys (Meleagris gallopavo)," *Poultry Science* 92, no. 6 (2013): 1467–73. doi:10.3382/ps.2012-02943.

p. 33: The proportion of time wild turkeys spend foraging is estimated in William M. Healy, "Behavior," in *The Wild Turkey: Biology and Management*, ed. James G. Dickson (Mechanicsburg, PA: Stackpole Books, 1992), 46–65. The welfare issues arising for confined turkeys are outlined in Marisa Erasmus, "Welfare Issues in Turkey Production," in *Advances in Poultry Welfare*, ed. Joy Mench (Cambridge, UK: Woodhead Publishing, 2018), 263–91.

p. 36: Jacquie Jacob discusses "Beak Trimming of Poultry," for the USDA Poultry Extension Service at https://poultry.extension.org/articles/poultry-behavior/beak-trimming-of-poultry/, accessed March 6, 2024. On the pain this procedure causes, see "FAWC Opinion on Beak Trimming of Laying

Hens," Farm Animal Welfare Council, UK government, November 17, 2007, https://www.gov.uk.government/publications/fawc-opinion-on-beak-trimming-of-laying-hens; Upasana Verma, O. P. Dinani, Sharad Mishra, A. K. Santra, V. N. Khune, Nishma Singh, and Rupal Pathak, "Beak Trimming: A Management Tool," *Poultry Punch*, January 20, 2020, https://thepoultrypunch.com/2020/01/beak-trimming-a-management-tool.

p. 37: On the painful nature of partial toe amputation, see M. J. Gentle and L. H. Hunter, "Neural Consequences of Partial Toe Amputation in Chickens," *Research in Veterinary Science* 45, no. 3 (1988): 374–76. On the impact of the amputations on movement, see J. Fournier, K. Schwean-Lardner, T. D. Knezacek, S. Gomis, and H. L. Classen, "The Effect of Toe Trimming on Behavior, Mobility, Toe Length and Other Indicators of Welfare in Tom Turkeys," *Poultry Science* 94, no. 7 (July 1, 2015): 1446–53; J. Fournier, K. Schwean-Lardner, T. D. Knezacek, S. Gomis, and H. L. Classen, "The Effect of Toe Trimming on Production Characteristics of Heavy Turkey Toms," *Poultry Science* 93, no. 9 (July 7, 2014): 2370–74.

p. 41: For the video referred to, with extracts from the investigator's diary, see https://pardonaturkey.com/.

p. 42: Information on stocking densities and the frequency of shed cleaning is available from the US

Poultry Industry Manual—Turkey Finishing,"
Poultry Site, November 24, 2022, https://www
.thepoultrysite.com/articles/turkey-finishing. On
the comparative sizes of wild and commercially
raised turkeys, see William M. Healy, "Behavior," in
The Wild Turkey: Biology and Management, ed. James
G. Dickson (Mechanicsburg, PA: Stackpole Books,
1992), 46–65; Kim Ha, "Talking Turkey," USDA, December 11, 2019, https://www.usda.gov/media/blog
/2019/12/11/talking-turkey.

p. 46: For the problems arising from breeding chick-
ens and turkeys to put on weight so fast, see James
Erlichman, "The Meat Factory: Cruel Cost of Cheap
Pork and Poultry—Factory Methods Have Slashed
Meat Prices in the Last 30 Years," *Guardian*, October
14, 1991; John Webster, *Animal Welfare: A Cool Eye
towards Eden* (Oxford: Blackwell Science, 1995), 156;
Virginie Allain, D. Huonnic, M. Rouina, and Virginie
Michel, "Prevalence of Skin Lesions in Turkeys at
Slaughter," *British Poultry Science* 54, no. 1 (2013):
33–41. For the recommendation of fast-growing
strains despite "the loss of a few birds," see R. Scott
Beyer, "Leg Problems in Broilers and Turkeys," Kansas State University, June 2004, https://krex.kstate
.edu/handle/2097/21686.

p. 47: The calculation of the number of birds is based
on figures in "US Poultry Industry Manual—Turkey

Finishing," Poultry Site, November 24, 2022, https://
www.thepoultrysite.com/articles/turkey-finishing;
Kim Ha, "Talking Turkey," USDA, December 11,
2019, https://www.usda.gov/media/blog/2019/12
/11/talking-turkey. On breast blisters in turkeys,
see Edgar Oviedo-Rondón, "Predisposing Factors
That Affect Walking Ability in Turkeys and Broilers,"
Poultry Site, February 1, 2009, www.thepoultrysite
.com/articles/predisposing-factors-that-affect
-walking-ability-in-turkeys-and-broilers#; "Pre-
venting Breast Blisters and Buttons," Hybrid, January 5, 2022, www.hybridturkeys.com/en/news
/preventing-breast-blisters-and-buttons/.

p. 51: The desperate hunger of the parents of fast-growing chickens is apparent in M. Zukiwsky, Moham-
mad Afrouziyeh, F. E. Robinson, and Martin Zuidhof,
"Feeding, Feed-Seeking Behavior, and Reproductive
Performance of Broiler Breeders under Conditions
of Relaxed Feed Restriction," Poultry Science 100,
no. 1 (2021): 119–28, doi:10.1016/j.psj.2020.09.081.

p. 54: The Butterball video can be viewed at "Hidden Cam-
era: Shocking Truth behind Butterball Thanksgiving,"
Mercy for Animals, November 14, 2012, https://www
.facebook.com/watch/?v=434283839954515. On
the inadequacies of US federal legislation to protect farmed animals, see Animal Welfare Institute,
Legal Protections for Animals on Farms, May 2022,

https://awionline.org/sites/default/files/uploads/documents/22-Legal-Protections-Farm.pdf.

p. 56: The study of slaughterhouses in France and Spain was conducted by Alexandra Contreras-Jodar, Aranzazu Varvaró-Porter, Antonio Velarde, and Virginie Michel, and published as "Relevant Indicators of Consciousness after Waterbath Stunning in Turkeys and Stunning Efficiency in Commercial Conditions," *Animals* 13, no. 4 (2023): 668, doi:10.3390/ani13040668.

p. 57: Timothy Pachirat refers to the high turnover rate among slaughterhouse workers in *Every Twelve Seconds* (New Haven, CT: Yale University Press, 2011), 85–86. See also Björn Jóhann Ólafsson, "The Human Cost of Working in a Slaughterhouse," *jfa*, January 16, 2023, https://www.thejfa.com/read/human-cost-working-slaughterhouse. Butterball's claims about its product are made in its advice on "How to Choose a Turkey," accessed March 11, 2024, https://www.butterball.com/how-to/choose-a-turkey. For what the PETA investigator recorded, see "Turkeys Used for Food," PETA, accessed March 11, 2024, https://www.peta.org/issues/animals-used-for-food/factory-farming/turkeys/.

pp. 63–65: I am indebted to Crystal Heath for allowing me access to the Minnesota veterinary reports on "depopulations" obtained via state public records request, from which this information is drawn, and confirmation based on indemnity funding paid out by the USDA that the turkeys were produced for Jennie-O Turkey Store. Further details are available at https://www.ourhonor.org/blognew/bailouts. For the use of the term "euthanize" to describe heating birds to death, see Kim Bellware, "Egg Prices Haven't Come Down with Inflation. Here's Why," *Washington Post*, January 10, 2023; Sue Willson, "Live Bird Farms Ordered to Euthanize Healthy Flocks Due to Potential Spread of Avian Flu," ABC27, WHTM, February 24, 2023, https://www.abc27.com/news/top-stories/live -bird-farms-ordered-to-euthanize-healthy-flocks -due-to-potential-spread-of-avian-flu/.

p. 65: See the USDA report, "2022–2023 Highly Pathogenic Avian Influenza Outbreak," www.aphis.usda. gov/sites/default/files/hpai-2022-2023-summary -depop-analysis.pdf. For the number of days taken to "secondary depopulation," see Figure 12. The killing of pigs by VSD+ is described, in a tone that is objective and yet horrifying, by the veterinarians who supervised it, Angela Baysinger, Michael Senn, Jordan Gebhardt, Christopher Rademacher, and Monique Pairis-Garcia, in "A Case Study of Ventilation Shutdown with the Addition of High Temperature and Humidity for Depopulation of Pigs," *Journal of the American Veterinary Medical Association* 259, no. 4 (August 2021): 415–24. On the continuing use of VSD+ for chickens, see Gwendolen Reyes-Illg, Jessica E. Martin, Indu Mani, James Reynolds, and Barry Kipperman, "The Rise of Heatstroke as a Method of Depopulating Pigs and Poultry: Implications for the US Veterinary Profession," *Animals* 13, no. 1 (2023): 140, doi:10.3390/ani13010140. For continuing outbreaks of HPAI in 2024, see *WattPoultry*, May 6, 2024, https://www.wattagnet.com/poultry-meat/diseases-health/avian-influenza/article/15670187/minnesota-has-second-commercial-flock-hit-by-hpai-in-2024. The 2010 study showing rapid death from nitrogen foam is: UK Department for Environment, Food & Rural Affairs, "Further study to develop a humane method to kill poultry using gas-filled foam - MH0144, https://randd.defra.gov.uk/ProjectDetails?ProjectId=16822.

p. 67: The reports referred to from the European Food Safety Authority Panel on Animal Health and Welfare are "Killing for Purposes Other Than Slaughter: Poultry," scientific opinion adopted September 26, 2019, *EFSA Journal* 17, no. 11 (2019): 5850; "Welfare of Pigs during Killing for Purposes Other Than Slaughter," scientific opinion adopted June 25, 2020, *EFSA Journal* 18, no. 7 (2020): 6195.

p. 70: The veterinarians quoted in this paragraph about the AVMA's acceptance of VSD+ provided their views to Crystal Heath in 2023, with permission for them to be used publicly.

p. 72: Information on the financial compensation received by turkey producers is drawn from USDA Animal Plant and Health Inspection Service payments, which can be obtained by searching https://www.usaspend ing.gov. Our Honor has compiled this information and made it available at: https://www.ourhonor.org /blognew/bailouts.

p. 75: For my defense of the principle of equal consideration of interests, see Peter Singer, *Animal Liberation* (New York: New York Review of Books, 1975); Peter Singer, *Animal Liberation Now* (New York: Harper-Collins, 2023).

p. 78: Here are the most relevant works of the thinkers mentioned: Tom Regan, *The Case for Animal Rights* (Berkeley: University of California Press, 2004); Christine Korsgaard, *Fellow Creatures* (Oxford: Oxford University Press, 2018); Martha Nussbaum, *Justice for Animals* (New York: Simon and Schuster, 2022); Andrew Linzey, *Animal Rights* (London: S.C.M. Press, 1976); David Clough, *On Animals* (New York: Bloomsbury, 2014); Charles Camosy, *For Love of Animals* (Cincinnati: Franciscan Media, 2013); Peter Singer and Shih Chao-Hwei, *The Buddhist and the Ethicist* (Boulder, CO: Shambhala, 2023).

About the Author

Peter Singer is professor emeritus of bio-ethics at Princeton University and has been described as the world's most influential philosopher. His many books include *Animal Liberation*, *Practical Ethics*, *The Life You Can Save*, and *Ethics in the Real World* (Princeton).

Also by Peter Singer

PRINCETON UNIVERSITY PRESS

Available wherever books are sold